Should I Pray?

or

Should I Worry?

Written and Illustrated
by Emily Moon

ISBN: 979-8-9939565-1-0

heymrsmoon.com

Dedicated to: Grandma Gail

Thank you for always being a
Christian role model to me and
so many others.

Either learn to pray, or become good at worrying! What you give to God, He handles. What you keep, you handle.

-Author Unknown

The Bible says to *pray always* . God is always listening! He always hears our prayers. But what does it look like to pray all the time?

Write or draw a picture of your favorite place to pray.

Thank You, God,

for the sun in the sky.

Thank You, God,

for the birds way up high.

Thank You, God,

for the rain falling down.

Thank You, God,

for the rocks rough or round.

Thank You, God,

for my mom and my dad.

Thank You, God,

for my siblings so rad.

Thank You, God,

for the flowers that bloom.

Thank You, God,

for my bike that goes zoom.

Thank You, God,

for creating me.

Thank You, God,

for all that I see!

Write or draw a picture thanking God for someone or something.

Now, days aren't always sunny, smiles, and wins.
So what do I do if
I struggle to grin?

Write or draw a picture of a person or pet who makes you smile when you are sad.

Lord, please help me be brave

in my dark room.

I know You are with me

morning, night, and noon.

Lord, please help me to listen

at home and at school.

You gave me two ears and

a brain that are cool.

Lord, please comfort me
when I am sad.
You are right there beside me,
even if I'm not glad.
Lord, please help me
when I have a tough day.
Let Your will be done
as I work and I play.

Lord, please help me and my family feel better when sick.

You are our Healer and can strengthen us quick.

Lord, please help me to always do my best.

And to You I will always leave the rest.

Write or draw a picture of your favorite food when you are sick.

Lord, You always listen

when I pray,

and the Holy Spirit helps

when I have

no words to say.

Draw a picture of you praying.

Now what if I do something wrong?

Will God's love and mercy be gone?

God's love and mercy

will never run out.

Ask for forgiveness and He'll show

you what He's all about!

I'm sorry for hurting my

friend today.

Please help me to only be kind

while we play.

I'm sorry for not doing what

mom and dad ask.

Please help me to obey

and finish the task.

Draw a picture of what you like to play with your friends.

I'm sorry for lying,

I know You know all.

Please help me tell the truth

no matter how big

or how small.

I'm sorry for stealing,

I know that was bad.

Please help me be grateful

for all that I have.

Thank You, Jesus, for dying on

the cross;

rising again, taking our sin,

and finding the lost.

No matter what happens, or

time of day, we can always

talk to God and

pray, pray, pray!

He loves you.

He sees you.

He's with you wherever you go.

Keep praying, keep talking,

God loves you just so.

Write or draw your own prayer, thanking God for always loving you and seeing you.

_____

_____

_____

_____

_____

_____

_____

_____

_____

_____

_____

_____

_____

Either learn to pray,
or become good at
worrying! What you
give to God, He
handles. What you
keep, you handle.
-Author Unknown